T0069714

Eggs in the Hay

Clive Percival
Illustrated by Andrew Plant

How many eggs are in the hay?
How many eggs will hatch today?

The first egg cracks.
Mother duck quacks.

Look! One little duckling!

The second egg cracks.
Mother duck quacks.

Look! Two little ducklings!

The third egg cracks.
Mother duck quacks.

Look! Three little ducklings!

The fourth egg cracks.
Mother duck quacks.

Look! Four little ducklings!

How many eggs were in the hay?
How many ducklings hatched today?